Learn Japanese Vocabulary through Memes

Clay & Yumi Boutwell

Copyright ©2021 Kotoba Books

www.TheJapanShop.com
www.TheJapanesePage.com
www.MakotoPlus.com

All rights reserved.

INTRODUCTION

Vocabulary through memes

Memes. They are everywhere these days. A meme is most often an humorous image with text that is spread rapidly by internet users. We think funny memes can be a good way to learn vocabulary and Japanese sentence structure.

The memes found in this collection were posted on our Instagram over the past few years. If you like this kind of humor (the few, the brave), please follow us:

https://www.instagram.com/thejapanshop/

The sentences found in this collection may or may not be beginner level, but every word and grammar point is explained so even beginners can understand. Nearly all examples are very casual, and while mostly suitable for using around friends, it isn't recommended for use with people you've just met.

If you find a sentence you like, try memorizing it so you can plug and play other words to use the form in different contexts. The sentences are short and represent natural Japanese you may not find in regular Japanese textbooks.

Japanese Pronunciation

As a quick and dirty guide, pronounce the consonants as you would in English. The vowels are like the vowel sounds in Spanish. a (ah); i (ii); u (oo); e (eh); o (oh)

See the last page to download sound files for all the Japanese found in the book.

ABOUT CLAY & YUMI

Yumi was a popular radio DJ in Japan for over ten years. She has extensive training in standard Japanese pronunciation which makes her perfect for creating these language instructional audio files.

Clay has been a passionate learner of Japanese for over twenty years now. His free language learning website, www.TheJapanesePage.com, got its start back in 1999 as a way to help other learners of Japanese as well as himself.

In 2002, they opened www.TheJapanShop.com to help students of Japanese get hard-to-find Japanese books.

Yumi and I are **very grateful** for your purchase and we truly hope this book will help you improve your Japanese. **We love our customers and don't take a single one of you for granted.** If you have any questions about this book or Japanese in general, I invite you to contact us below by

email or on social media.

Clay & Yumi Boutwell (and Makoto & Megumi) in Fukui, Japan
help@thejapanshop.com

@theJapanShop

www.facebook.com/LearningJapaneseatTheJapanShop

http://www.TheJapanShop.com
http://www.TheJapanesePage.com
www.MakotoPlus.com

Become a Makoto+ member right now!

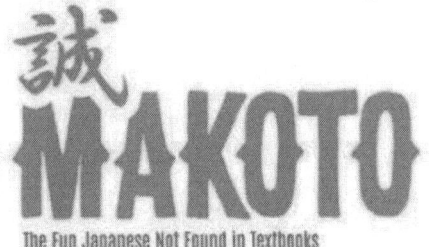

Japanese lessons and stories with sound files.

It's only a few bucks a month!
https://www.thejapanesepage.com/makoto

You'll get:
Download the Latest Makoto Issue | Read 3 Full Back Issues Online | Reusable TheJapanShop.com Coupon | Exclusive Lessons & Content

FOR BEGINNERS TO INTERMEDIATES

Table of Contents
INTRODUCTION 2

1: And where is today's tribute? 9

2: Today was fun as always 11

3: Good-looking Guy 13

4: Now, where did I put the keys? 15

5: That was delicious 17

6: It's a little ticklish, but I'll endure 20

7: Looks delicious 22

8: Juvenile Delinquent Llama 24

9: Who won? I did! 26

11: To have a terrible time 30

12: Where's the party? 32

13: Again... no furigana! 34

14: Whenever I see kanji, I lose heart. 36

15: When will you go home? I'm always a frog. 38

16: At last, I remembered the correct stroke order! 40

17: He's got three priors. 42

18: I'm going to study Japanese hard today! 44

19: Without my glasses, I can't see anything. Who are you? 46

20: Diet? That starts tomorrow. 49

21: Earthlings. we require the use of your toilet. ASAP!! 51

22: Today is the day I'm going to float. 53

23: CAT: What? Are you an idiot? DOG: Amazing. You are a genius. 55

24: You wanna morning kiss, don't you? 57

25: I'm so happy to have an acorn. 59

26: The next breadcrumb is mine. Got it? 61

27: Hey, let's go somewhere for the May holidays! Can't. No money. 63

28: It wasn't me. It was the cat. C-A-T! 66

29: Come out and play with me! 68

30: You still don't wanna play today? 70

31: No matter how much I think about it, I don't get it. 72

32: Oh, is that so? 74

33: Don't take a picture without my makeup! 76

34: I can't resist sweets. 78

35: Has the meeting already started? 80

36: Is there a dolphin? 82

37: A fateful encounter 84

38: Finally, I'm off tomorrow. 86

39: Showing no sign of remorse or regret 88

40: The real culprit was the cat. 90

41: Planning a conspiracy 92

42: Um? Can I help you with something? 94

43: It's a tragedy. 96

44: Cut it out. It's embarrassing. 98

45: Motivated; let's play! 100

46: Unmotivated; no will to get moving; good grief 102

47: What should we do now? 104

48: Not amused. Hurry up with the catnip. 106

49: I'm a good looking guy. Best regards! 108

50: Anyway, hurry up and kiss me. - The prince who turned into a frog 110

DOWNLOAD LINK 113

1: And where is today's tribute?

> # 今日の貢ぎ物は？
>
> *kyou no mitsugi mono wa?*
> today | 's | tribute | as for?
> And where is today's tribute?

BREAK IT DOWN:

- 今日の【きょうの】today's

- 貢ぎ物【みつぎもの】tribute [In addition to historical tributes between states, this is used today in a religious context (gift to God) or societal (gift to boss; gift to yakuza boss) or with sarcasm; often used with this verb: 貢ぎ物を捧げます]

- は [this is the topic marker. It indicates there is something unspoken: "Where is it?"]

NOTES:

Ending a sentence with a questioning は is fairly common in spoken Japanese. If someone asks you a question such as "How are you?" or "Are you going to the party?" you can return the question with a あなたは？ And you?

2: Today was fun as always

今日も楽しかった。

kyou mo tanoshikatta
today | also | was fun
Today was fun as always

BREAK IT DOWN:

- 今日【きょう】today

- も also [implies past days were also fun]

- 楽しかった【たのしかった】was fun [past of 楽しい (fun; enjoyable)]

NOTES:

Unlike English, adjectives are conjugated in Japanese. 楽しい is an -I adjective which is conjugated like this:
楽し<u>い</u> (fun; enjoyable) [the plain form retains the い]
楽し<u>かった</u> (was fun) [drop the い and add かった]
楽し<u>くない</u> (isn't fun) [drop the い and add くない]
楽し<u>くなかった</u> (was not fun) [drop the い and add くなかった]

3: Good-looking Guy

> # 僕ってイケメンだと思わない？
>
> *boku tte ikemen da to omowanai?*
> I; me | (quotation) | good looking guy | am | don't you think?
> I'm not bad in the looks department, don't you think?

BREAK IT DOWN:

- 僕【ぼく】 I; me

- って as for (me); casual quoting particle

- イケメン handsome; good-looking guy

- だ is; am [simple of です]

- と (quoting particle)

- 思わない？【おもわない】 don't (you) think?

NOTES:

The って is an informal quoting particle. It may imply a supposition: if ... then ...

4: Now, where did I put the keys?

> 鍵(かぎ)はどこに置(お)いたかな。
>
> *kagi wa doko ni oita kana.*
> key | as for | where | at | placed | I wonder?
> Now, where did I put the keys?

BREAK IT DOWN:

- 鍵【かぎ】 key
- は (topic marker)
- どこに (to) where
- 置いた【おいた】 placed; put
- かな I wonder

NOTES:

Japanese has many sentence enders such as かな to show questioning, emphasis, emotion, confidence, and uncertainty.

5: That was delicious

おいしかった。猫(ねこ)のフン、
ちょうど欲(ほ)しかった。

oishikatta. neko no fun, choudo hoshikatta..
was delicious | cat | 's | poop | just | wanted
That was delicious. I've been wanting cat poop.

BREAK IT DOWN:

- おいしかった was delicious [past of おいしい (delicious)]

- 猫 cat

- フン poop

- 猫のフン cat's poop [the の limits the information: not just any poop but a cat's poop]

- ちょうど just; precisely; right

- 欲しかった wanted [past of ほしい (want)]

- ちょうど欲しかった I've been wanting...; just what I wanted

NOTES:

ちょうど欲しかった is a useful expression to use when receiving a gift from someone. "I've been wanting that."

Unless you have both cats and dogs, you may not get this joke. Most dogs like the taste of cat poop due to the high-fat content of cat food.

We apologize for the image now stuck in your head.

6: It's a little ticklish, but I'll endure

ちょっと、くすぐったい
けど、我慢(がまん)

It's a little ticklish, but... I'll endure.

chotto kusuguttai kedo, gaman.

> ちょっと、くすぐったいけど、
> 我慢(がまん)。
>
> *chotto, kusuguttai kedo, gaman.*
> A little | ticklish | but | perseverance
> **It's a little ticklish, but... I'll endure.**

BREAK IT DOWN:

- ちょっと a little
- くすぐったい ticklish
- けど but; however
- 我慢 endurance; to bear with; perseverance

NOTES:

Like がんばる (to do one's best; to keep at it), the concept of 我慢(がまん) is thoroughly Japanese. It seems Japanese are either 頑張る-ing or 我慢-ing or both.

7: Looks delicious

> はらへった。うまそう、おまえ。
>
> *harahetta. umasou, omae.*
> stomach | decreased | looks delicious | you
> **I'm starving. Looks delicious. You.**

BREAK IT DOWN:

- はらへった hungry [literally this is stomach is decreased 腹減った and is a common, casual way to say "I'm hungry"]

- うまそう looks delicious [the そう means "looks like"]

- おまえ you [can be rude]

NOTES:

Japanese has more flexibility with the positioning of words than in English. The オチ *ochi* is the punchline of a joke. Since you can play with the position of words, it can be funny or powerful to drop the main thought last. In this case, おまえ (you) is the unexpected word that brings home the meaning.

8: Juvenile Delinquent Llama

不良少年ラマ。

furyou shounen rama.
bad | youth | llama

Juvenile delinquent Llama

BREAK IT DOWN:

- 不良【ふりょう】 bad; hoodlum [literally, not good]
- 少年【しょうねん】 boy; youth; juvenile; lad
- 不良少年【ふりょうしょうねん】 juvenile delinquent
- ラマ llama

NOTES:

In Japanese, it is common to stack adjectives, verb phrases, or noun phrases before nouns. This gives us more detail about the noun. In this case, it tells us the llama is a bad youth. Here are a few other possibilities:

- 目が見えないラマ a llama that can't see
- 髪が長いラマ a llama with long hair
- 日本語を勉強するラマ a llama that studies Japanese

9: Who won? I did!

> # 誰が勝った？俺だ！
>
> *dare ga katta? ore da!*
> who | (subject marker) | won? | I | did
>
> **Who won? I did!**

BREAK IT DOWN:

- 誰が【だれが】 who (was the one) [誰 (who) が (indicates the doer of the action)]
- 勝った【かった】 won [past of 勝つ【かつ】 (to win)]
- 俺【おれ】 I; me [male pronoun; somewhat rude; not something a child would say!]
- だ did [simple of です]

NOTES:

This sentence is very casual. Notice it not only uses the plain past form of the verb, but it also doesn't have a question particle. This is common in casual, spoken Japanese.

10: My dream is... world domination

ぼくの夢(ゆめ)は・・・
世界(せかい)征服(せいふく)

My dream is... world domination.

boku no yume wa... sekai seifuku

> ## ぼくの夢は・・・世界征服
>
> *boku no yume wa... sekai seifuku*
> my | dream | as for | world | conquest; subjugation
>
> **My dream is... world domination.**

BREAK IT DOWN:

- ぼくの my [ぼく (I; me); の (limiter; possessive)]

- 夢【ゆめ】dream

- は as for [topic marker]

- 世界【せかい】world; society

- 征服【せいふく】conquest; domination

NOTES:

Japanese has a large number of pronouns to choose from. ぼく is common for men—especially younger men, but wouldn't be used by a super strong man wanting to take over the world. So, when this cute and tiny chipmonk uses ぼく it makes the end of the sentence all the more comical.

11: To have a terrible time

えらい目にあう
to have a terrible time

erai me ni au

えらい目にあう。

erai me ni au
great; terrible | eye | to | meet

To have a terrible time

BREAK IT DOWN:

- えらい awful; terrible [this is an emphasizing word that normally means something positive: great; excellent; remarkable; etc.]

- 目にあう to go through; to experience; to suffer [literally, "to meet (one's) eye"]

NOTES:

This is a very common and useful idiom to use when you've had a bad time.

12: Where's the party?

> # パーティーはどこでやっているの？
>
> *pa-ti- wa doko de yatte iru no?*
> party | as for | where | at | doing | ?
>
> **Where's the party?**

BREAK IT DOWN:

- パーティー party
- は as for (topic marker)
- どこ where
- で at (where)
- やっている happening; doing [the ている form indicates a continual action]
- の (question ender) [rising tone]

NOTES:

As you learn vocabulary words, pay attention to the enlongated sounds. Remembering which words have long sounds will greatly help with your pronunciation.

13: Again... no furigana!

> また、ふりがながない！
>
> *mata, furigana ga nai*
> again | furigana | doesn't exist
>
> **Again... no furigana!**

BREAK IT DOWN:

- また again

- ふりがな furigana (the small hiragana above kanji to help with reading)

- がない doesn't exist; isn't; not

NOTES:

Your goal should be to wean yourself off furigana. Once you get to the upper beginner stage, it might be a good idea to set aside a year mainly to focus on learning kanji. Studying a few kanji a day with systems such as Kodansha's Kanji Learner's Course or Heisig's Remembering the Kanji may be helpful.

14: Whenever I see kanji, I lose heart.

> 漢字を見るとがっかりします。
>
> *kanji o miru to gakkari shimasu.*
> kanji | (direct object marker) | upon seeing | to be disappointed; dejected
>
> **Whenever I see kanji, I lose heart.**

BREAK IT DOWN:

- 漢字【かんじ】kanji; Chinese characters
- を (direct object marker)
- 見ると【みると】upon seeing [見る (to see) + と (upon; and then...)]
- がっかりします to be disappointed

NOTES:

Japanese is full of words like がっかり that describe an emotional state with almost onomatopoeic words.

15: When will you go home? I'm always a frog.

いつ、かえる？

When will you go home?

ぼく、いつも かえる。
I'm always a frog.

itsu kaeru? boku itsumo kaeru.

> いつ、かえる？ぼく、いつもかえる。
>
> *itsu kaeru? boku itsumo kaeru.*
> when | return | I | always | frog
>
> **When will you go home? I'm always a frog.**

BREAK IT DOWN:

- いつ when
- かえる return; go home [帰る]
- ぼく I; me
- いつも always
- かえる frog [usually written in katakana カエル]

NOTES:

This entry could rightly be called an 親父ギャグ (old man's gag or dad joke). When someone says a joke as lame as this one, you can respond by saying, 「さむっ！」 and rubbing your arms as if you are cold. さむい literally, cold, is said when a joke falls flat or is just too lame.

16: At last, I remembered the correct stroke order!

やっと正しい書き順覚えた！

I finally remembered the correct stroke order!

yatto tadashii kakijun oboeta

> やっと正しい書き順覚えた！
>
> yatto tadashii kakijun oboeta
>
> finally | correct | stroke order | remembered
>
> **At last, I remembered the correct stroke order!**

BREAK IT DOWN:

- やっと finally; at last

- 正しい【ただしい】correct

- 書き順【かきじゅん】(kanji or kana) stroke order

- 覚えた【おぼえた】remembered; memorized [past of 覚える (to remember; to learn by heart)]

NOTES:

It isn't nearly as important these days to learn to write Japanese as it was, say, in the 1980s. How often do you hand-write English? However, take the time to learn the rules of Japanese stroke order. It will help you write neatly and you'll earn respect for doing things properly.

17: He's got three priors.

彼(かれ)は前科(ぜんか)三犯(さんぱん)だ

He's got three priors.

kare wa zenka sanpan da

> # 彼は前科三犯だ。
>
> *kare wa zenka sanpan da*
> he | as for | criminal record | 3 crimes | has
>
> **He's got three priors.**

BREAK IT DOWN:

- 彼【かれ】he

- は as for [topic marker]

- 前科【ぜんか】criminal record; previous conviction

- 三犯【さんぱん】3 priors; 3 crimes

- だ has [simple form of copula です]

NOTES:

You may recognize the counter for crimes 犯 from 犯人 (criminal).

18: I'm going to study Japanese hard today!

今日(きょう)はしっかり日本語(にほんご)を勉強(べんきょう)します！

I'm going to study Japanese hard today!

kyou wa shikkari nihongo o benkyou shimasu!

> 今日はしっかり日本語を勉強します！
>
> *kyou wa shikkari nihongo o benkyou shimasu!*
> today | as for | firmly; fully | Japanese language | (will) study
>
> **I'm going to study Japanese hard today!**

BREAK IT DOWN:

- 今日【きょう】today
- は as for (topic marker)
- しっかり properly; hard (studying); firmly; fully
- 日本語【にほんご】Japanese language
- を (direct object marker)
- 勉強します【べんきょう】to study

NOTES:

This is a great phrase to recite every morning when you wake up! しっかり means she will skip no corners. She will study fully and correctly.

19: Without my glasses, I can't see anything. Who are you?

メガネがないと何も見えない。
あんた誰？

Without my glasses, I can't see anything. Who are you?

- メガネ eyeglasses
- がない without; no (glasses)
- と and [cause and effect: without glasses ... can't see]
- 何も【なにも】 nothing [used with a negative verb]
- 見えない【みえない】 can't see; unable to see [past potential of 見る (to see)]
- あんた you [can be rude; use あなた instead]
- 誰【だれ】 who

www.TheJapanShop.com/vocab

> メガネがないと何も見えない。
>
> あんた誰？
>
> *megane ga nai to nanimo mienai. anta dare?*
> glasses | (subject marker) | don't have | and | nothing | can't see | you | who?
>
> **Without my glasses, I can't see anything. Who are you?**

BREAK IT DOWN:

- メガネ eyeglasses

- がない without; no (glasses)

- と and [cause and effect: without glasses ... can't see]

- 何も【なにも】 nothing [used with a negative verb]

- 見えない【みえない】 can't see; unable to see [past potential of 見る (to see)]

- あんた you [can be rude; use あなた instead]

- 誰【だれ】 who

NOTES:

Usually, when you see a word in katakana, it is a foreign loanword. But メガネ (eyeglasses) is actually 眼鏡 (eye – mirror). Some non-loanwords may be written in katakana for:
- emphasis
- kanji is too difficult or not common
- personal choice

20: Diet? That starts tomorrow.

ダイエットは明日(あした)からね。
Diet? That starts tomorrow.

- ダイエット diet
- 明日 tomorrow
- から from (tomorrow)
- ね right? you know... (ender showing confidence or emphasis)

> ダイエットは明日からね。
>
> *daietto wa ashita kara ne..*
> diet | as for | tomorrow | from | you know
>
> **Diet? That starts tomorrow.**

BREAK IT DOWN:

- ダイエット diet
- 明日 tomorrow
- から from (tomorrow)
- ね right? you know... (ender showing confidence or emphasis)

NOTES:

English loanwords written in katakana can be surprisingly tricky to remember. In this case, remember to add that pause or space with the small っ.

English speakers tend to neglect practicing the Japanese pronunciation of English loanwords and this leads to bad pronunciation.

21: Earthlings. we require the use of your toilet. ASAP!!

地球人よ、大至急、トイレ貸して！！

Earthlings. we require the use of your toilet. ASAP!!

- 地球人【ちきゅうじん】 earthling [literally, "earth people"]
- よ (emphatic; has the effect of "listen up!" as if speaking to inferiors)
- 大至急【だいしきゅう】ASAP]
- トイレ toilet; bathroom
- 貸して【かして】 lend (command) [from 貸す (to lend)]

> 地球人よ、大至急、トイレ貸して！！
>
> *chikyuujin yo daishikyuu toire kashite!*
> earth person | (emphatic attention grabber) | ASAP | toilet | lend (us)
>
> **Earthlings. we require the use of your toilet. ASAP!!**

BREAK IT DOWN:

- 地球人【ちきゅうじん】earthling [literally, "earth people"]

- よ (emphatic; has the effect of "listen up!" to get people's attention)

- 大至急【だいしきゅう】ASAP

- トイレ toilet; bathroom

- 貸して【かして】lend (command) [from 貸す (to lend)]

NOTES:

Add 人 (jin) after (most) locations: 火星人（かせいじん）(martian); ロシア人（じん）(Russian); 日本人（にほんじん）(Japanese)

22: Today is the day I'm going to float.

今日(きょう)こそ、浮(う)かんでみせるぞ！

Today is the day I'm going to float.

https://www.patreon.com/TheJapanesePage

> 今日こそ、浮かんでみせるぞ！
>
> *kyou koso, ukande miseru zo!*
> today | it is | float and | show (them)
>
> **Today is the day I'm going to float.**

BREAK IT DOWN:

- 今日【きょう】today

- こそ it is...; definitely [it is today... today is the day]

- 浮かんで【うかんで】 floating [て form of 浮かぶ【うかぶ】(to float)]

- みせる show; do [here, this is more self-talk; he is convincing himself today he will not sink.]

- ぞ (adds force)

NOTES:

Both こそ and ぞ show a detemination to do something.

23: CAT: What? Are you an idiot? DOG: Amazing. You are a genius.

【猫】何それ？馬鹿じゃないの
【犬】すごい。天才だ！

CAT: What? Are you an idiot? DOG: Amazing. You are a genius.

- 何それ【なにそれ】What? What's that? [used to show shock]
- 馬鹿【ばか】fool; idiot
- じゃないの aren't you? [じゃない (isn't) の (emotive question ender)]
- すごい amazing; wonderful; great
- 天才【てんさい】genius

> 【猫】何それ？馬鹿じゃないの
>
> 【犬】すごい。天才だ！
>
> *[neko] nani sore? baka janai no? [inu] sugoi. tensai da!*
> [cat] what | that | stupid | aren't (you) | question marker | [dog] | amazing | genius | are
>
> **CAT: What? Are you an idiot? DOG: Amazing. You are a genius.**

BREAK IT DOWN:

- 何それ【なにそれ】What? What's that? [used to show shock]
- 馬鹿【ばか】fool; idiot
- じゃないの aren't you? [じゃない (isn't) の (emotive question ender)]
- すごい amazing; wonderful; great
- 天才【てんさい】genius

NOTES:

While rude, it isn't uncommon to hear friends say, 「バカじゃないの？」 (Are you an idiot) which is literally, "Are you not an idiot?"

24: You wanna morning kiss, don't you?

おはようのキスがほしいんでしょ？
You wanna morning kiss, don't you?

- おはよう morning [this is the morning greeting but used here to mean "morning" in general]
- キス kiss
- おはようのキス morning kiss [parse from the back to front: kiss of morning]
- ほしい want; desire [takes the が particle]
- んでしょ don't you (want)? [the ん indicates the dog is pretty sure that's what the owner really wants.]

> おはようのキスがほしいんでしょ？
>
> *ohayou no kisu ga hoshiin desho?*
> morning | 's | kiss | (subject/object marker) | want | don't you?
>
> **You wanna morning kiss, don't you?**

BREAK IT DOWN:

- おはよう morning [this is the morning greeting but used here to mean "morning" in general]

- キス kiss

- おはようのキス morning kiss [parse from the back to front: kiss of morning]

- ほしい want; desire [takes the が particle]

- んでしょ don't you (want)? [the ん indicates the dog is pretty sure that's what the owner really wants.]

NOTES:

Other uses for キス: お休みのキス (goodnight kiss); さようならのキス (goodbye kiss); いってらっしゃいのキス (see you later kiss)

25: I'm so happy to have an acorn.

どんぐりがあるって幸せ[しあわ]。

I'm so happy to have an acorn.

- どんくり acorn
- がある have [が (subject/object marker) + ある (to have; to be)]
- って if..then [this is usually a quotation marker; here, it marks a cause and effect situation: having an acorn makes (me) happy]
- 幸せ【しあわせ】 happiness; good fortune; blessing

www.TheJapanShop.com/vocab

> # どんぐりがあるって幸せ。
>
> *donguri ga aru tte shiawase*
>
> acorn | (subject/object marker) | to have | is... (quotation marker) | happiness
>
> **Happieness is having an acorn.**

BREAK IT DOWN:

- どんぐり acorn
- ある to have
- って (casual quoting particle)
- 幸せ【しあわせ】happiness

NOTES:

Remember the difference between いる and ある. If it is not living or moving, use ある.

26: The next breadcrumb is mine. Got it?

つぎ　　　　　　　おれ
次のパンくずは俺の。わかった？

The next breadcrumb is mine. Got it?

- 次の【つぎの】 the next...
- パンくず breadcrumb
- は (topic marker; hiragana "ha" but pronounced "wa")
- 俺の mine
- わかった (do you) understand; understood?!

www.MakotoPlus.com | www.TheJapanesePage.com

> 次のパンくずは俺の。わかった？
>
> *tsugi no pan kuzu wa ore no. wakatta?*
> next | bread crumb | as for | mine | understood?
>
> **The next breadcrumb is mine. Got it?**

BREAK IT DOWN:

- 次の【つぎの】 the next...

- パンくず breadcrumb

- は (topic marker; hiragana "ha" but pronounced "wa")

- 俺の mine

- わかった (do you) understand; understood?!

NOTES:

わかった？ can mean, "Do you understand," but in this case, it is more like, "You understand and you will obey, won't you?"

27: Hey, let's go somewhere for the May holidays! Can't. No money.

ね、五月の連休にどこか行こうよ
(ごがつ　れんきゅう　　　い)

Hey, let's go somewhere for the May holidays!

だめ。お金ない
Can't. No money.

- ね hey
- 五月【ごがつ】 May [literally, fifth month]
- 連休に for the consecutive holidays [referring to Golden Week]
- どこか somewhere
- 行こうよ【いこうよ】 Let's go [the よ is an emphatic ender]

www.MakotoPlus.com

> ね、五月の連休にどこか行こうよ。
>
> だめ。お金ない。
>
> *ne, gogatsu no renkyuu ni doko ka ikou yo.*
>
> hey | May | 's | consecutive holidays | for | somewhere | let's go
>
> **Hey, let's go somewhere for the May holidays!
> Can't. No money.**

BREAK IT DOWN:

- ね hey

- 五月【ごがつ】May [literally, fifth month]

- 連休に for the consecutive holidays [referring to Golden Week]

- どこか somewhere

- 行こうよ【いこうよ】Let's go [the よ is an emphatic ender]

> NOTES:

The May holidays referred to here are called, "Golden Week" (ゴールデンウィーク). It is a series of holidays from April 29th to May 5th.

29 April
The Emperor's Birthday (天長節)
The Emperor's Birthday (天皇誕生日)
Greenery Day (みどりの日)
Shōwa Day (昭和の日)

3 May
Constitution Memorial Day (憲法記念日)

4 May
Citizen's Holiday (国民の休日)
Greenery Day (みどりの日)

5 May
Children's Day (子供の日), also known as Boys' Day or the Feast of Banners, traditionally celebrated as Tango no Sekku (端午の節句).

Data from Wikipedia:
https://en.wikipedia.org/wiki/Golden_Week_(Japan)

28: It wasn't me. It was the cat. C-A-T!

俺じゃない。猫だよ。ね・こ

おれ / ねこ

It wasn't me. It was the cat. The C-A-T!

- 俺【おれ】I; me [male speech]
- じゃない wasn't; not [casual of ではない]
- 猫【ねこ】cat
- だよ (emphatic ender: だ copula + よ for emphasis)

www.MakotoPlus.com

> 俺じゃない。猫だよ。ね・こ
>
> *ore janai. neko da yo. ne ko.*
> I | not | cat | (emphatic) | c a t
>
> **It wasn't me. It was the cat. C-A-T!**

BREAK IT DOWN:

- 俺【おれ】I; me [male speech]

- じゃない wasn't; not [casual of ではない]

- 猫【ねこ】cat

- だよ (emphatic ender: だ copula + よ for emphasis)

NOTES:

The dot between the hiragana indicates a slowed down pronunciation for emphasis.

29: Come out and play with me!

出てきて、ぼくと遊んでよ。
Come out and play with me!

- 出てきて【でてきて】 come out [compound of 出る (come out) and くる (to come); in compound words くる is often used to mean "do this and then come back"]
- ぼく I; me [mostly male language]
- と with (me)
- 遊んで【あそんで】 play (with me)
- よ (ender for emphasis)

> # 出てきて、ぼくと遊んでよ。
> *dete kite, boku to asonde yo.*
> out | come | me | with | play | (emphatic)
>
> **Come out and play with me!**

BREAK IT DOWN:

- ぼく I; me [mostly male language]
- と with (me)
- 遊んで【あそんで】 play (with me)
- よ (ender for emphasis)

NOTES:

Often, a kid will ask another kid to play by saying, 「あそぼう」 (let's play). Here, the cat is asking the same thing, but as a て form command.

30: You still don't wanna play today?

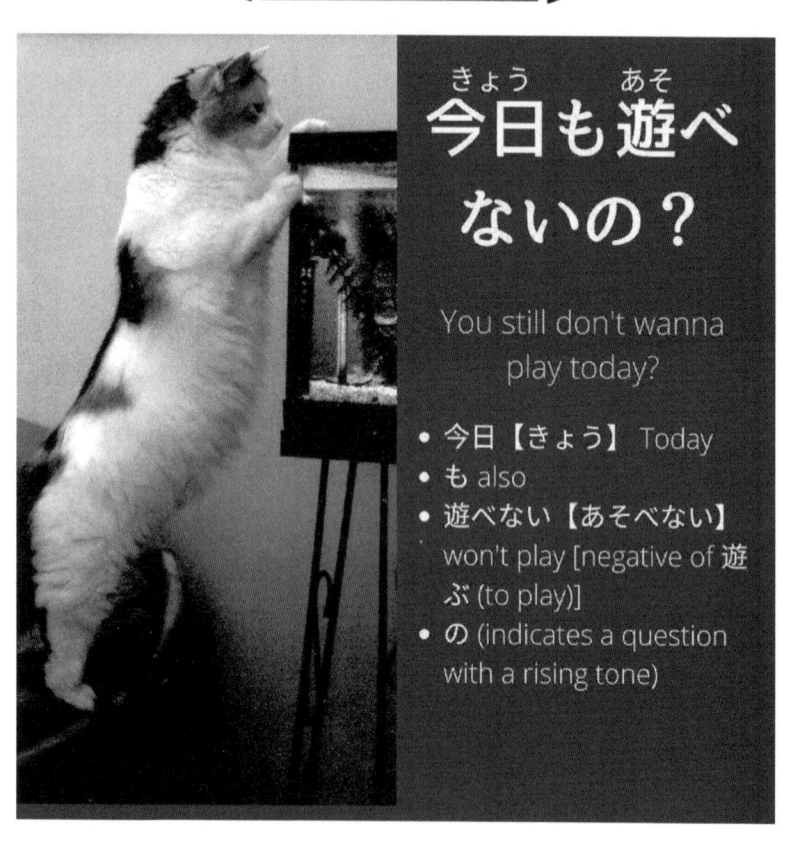

今日も遊べないの？

You still don't wanna play today?

- 今日【きょう】 Today
- も also
- 遊べない【あそべない】 won't play [negative of 遊ぶ (to play)]
- の (indicates a question with a rising tone)

> # 今日も遊べないの？
>
> *kyou mo asobenai no?*
> today | also | won't play | ?
>
> **You still don't wanna play today?**

BREAK IT DOWN:

- 今日【きょう】 today
- も also
- 遊べない【あそべない】 won't play
- の (informal question marker)

NOTES:

The の is used as a casual question marker like か. As in English, the tone at the end raises for a question.

31: No matter how much I think about it, I don't get it.

かんが
いくら考えてもわからない。

No matter how much I think about it, I don't get it.

- いくら however (much)
- 考えても even thinking [て form + も of 考える (to think)]
- いくら〜ても however much...
- わからない don't understand [from わかる (to understand)]

> # いくら考えてもわからない。
>
> *ikura kangaetemo wakaranai.*
> however much | thinking | even | don't understand
>
> **No matter how much I think about it, I don't get it.**

BREAK IT DOWN:

- いくら however (much)
- 考えても even thinking [て form + も of 考える (to think)]
- いくら〜ても however much...
- わからない don't understand [from わかる (to understand)]

NOTES:

The いくら〜ても is a useful form to learn:
- いくら電話をかけても通じません。 No matter how many times I call, it doesn't go through.
- 本はいくら読んでも読みすぎることはない。 You can never read too many books.

32: Oh, is that so?

へ〜、そうなんだぁ。
Oh, is that so?

- へえ〜 oh, really?
- そうなんだ that is so [often used in conversation as a question to show polite interest in the newly learned information]

> # へ〜、そうなんだぁ
>
> *hee, sou nan daa.*
> oh | so | what | is
>
> **Oh, is that so?**

BREAK IT DOWN:

- へえ〜 oh, really?

- そうなんだ that is so [often used in conversation as a question to show polite interest in the newly learned information]

NOTES:

This example is a form of あいづち (interjections indicating that one is paying attention). This is very common in conversational Japanese. へえ and some form of そう is especially common.

33: Don't take a picture without my makeup!

すっぴんだから、撮らないで！

Don't take a picture without my makeup!

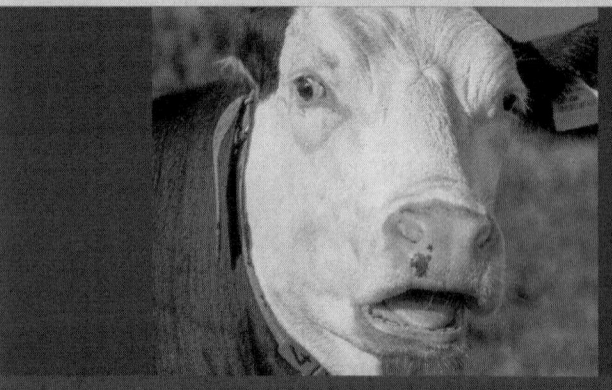

- すっぴん face with no makeup
- だから therefore; because of that
- 撮らないで【とらないで】 don't take (photo) [This kanji 撮 is used with taking photos or video]

> # すっぴんだから、撮らないで！
>
> *suppin dakara, toranaide!*
>
> no makeup face | therefore | don't take (photo)
>
> **Don't take a picture without my makeup!**

BREAK IT DOWN:

- すっぴん face with no makeup
- だから therefore; because of that
- 撮らないで【とらないで】 don't take (photo) [This kanji 撮 is used with taking photos or video]

NOTES:

Learning kanji early on will give you major benefits as you enter the intemediate stages. The word "to take" (*toru*) can use several kanji, but by choosing the correct one, the meaning is instantly understood even though the sounds are exactly the same:

- 撮る to take (a photo)
- 取る to take (general—most common form)
- 採る to pick (flowers); to take (a sample); to extract (juice)

34: I can't resist sweets.

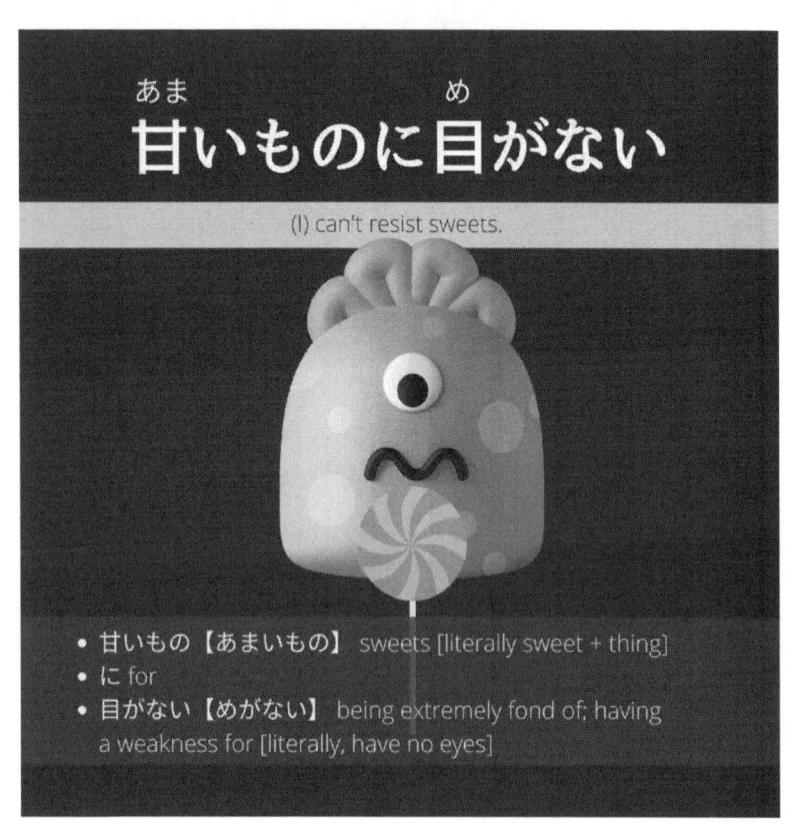

甘いものに目がない
あま　め

(I) can't resist sweets.

- 甘いもの【あまいもの】 sweets [literally sweet + thing]
- に for
- 目がない【めがない】 being extremely fond of; having a weakness for [literally, have no eyes]

> # 甘いものに目がない。
>
> *amai mono ni me ga nai.*
> sweet | thing | for | eye | doesn't exist
>
> **I can't resist sweets.**

BREAK IT DOWN:

- 甘いもの【あまいもの】 sweets [literally sweet + thing]
- に for
- 目がない【めがない】 being extremely fond of; having a weakness for [idiom; literally, have no eyes]

NOTES:

Learning idioms will greatly help your understanding and conversational abilities. They can also be fun. "no eye"?! It means you can't resist something.

35: Has the meeting already started?

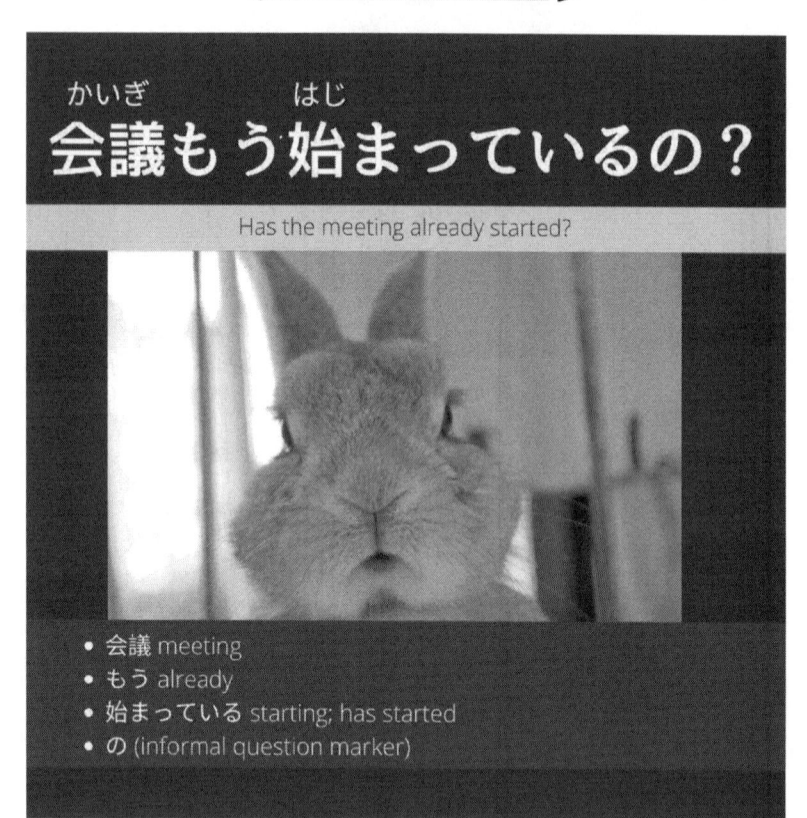

かいぎ　　　　　はじ
会議もう始まっているの？

Has the meeting already started?

- 会議 meeting
- もう already
- 始まっている starting; has started
- の (informal question marker)

> # 会議もう始まっているの？
>
> *kaigi mou hajimatte iru no?*
> meeting | already | staring | (question marker)
>
> **Has the meeting already started?**

BREAK IT DOWN:

- 会議 meeting
- もう already
- 始まっている starting; has started
- の (informal question marker)

NOTES:

This Zooming bunny thinks he's late for the meeting.
- もうはじまった already started
- もうおわった already finished

36: Is there a dolphin?

イルカいるか？

Is there a dolphin?

- イルカ dolphin
- いる exists; to be (animate objects)
- か (question)

A classic 親父ギャグ【おやじぎゃぐ】 (dad joke)

イルカいるか？

iruka iru ka?
dolphin | exists | (question marker)

Is there a dolphin?

BREAK IT DOWN:

- イルカ dolphin
- いる exists; to be (animate objects)
- か (question)

A classic 親父ギャグ【おやじぎゃぐ】 (dad joke)

NOTES:

We've included a few 親父ギャグ (dad jokes) in this collection. This is one of them. Playing on words is a favorite passtime of dads of any culture—even in Japan.

As mentioned previously, the correct response to something like this is, 「さむっ！」 (that's lame—literally, "cold")

37: A fateful encounter

運命の出会い
うんめい　であ

a fateful encounter

- 運命【うんめい】 fate; destiny
- の modifier particle: fateFUL encounter
- 出会い【であい】 meeting; rendezvous; encounter

This phrase is most often used in the romantic sense.

運命の出会い

unmei no deai
fate | 's | encounter

a fateful encounter

BREAK IT DOWN:

- 運命【うんめい】 fate; destiny
- の modifier particle: fateFUL encounter
- 出会い【であい】 meeting; rendezvous; encounter

This phrase is most often used in the romantic sense.

NOTES:

運命の is "fateful":

- 運命の皮肉 irony of fate [fateful irony]
- 運命のいたずら twist of fate [fateful prank]

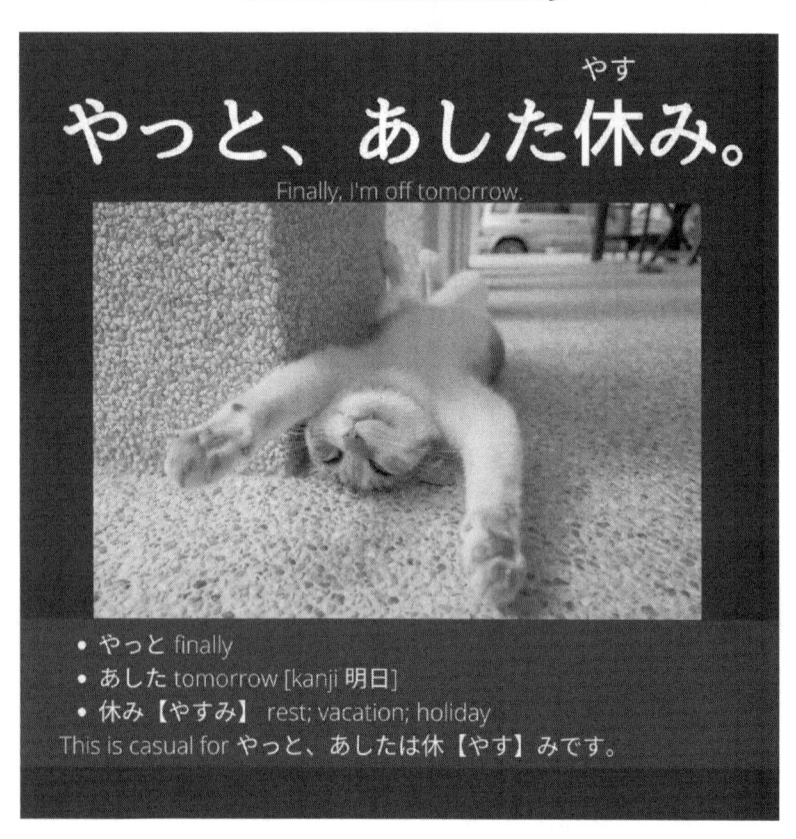

38: Finally, I'm off tomorrow.

やっと、あした休み。
Finally, I'm off tomorrow.

- やっと finally
- あした tomorrow [kanji 明日]
- 休み【やすみ】 rest; vacation; holiday

This is casual for やっと、あしたは休【やす】みです。

> やっと、あした休み。
>
> *yatto ashita yasumi.*
> finally | tomorrow | vacation
>
> **Finally, I'm off tomorrow.**

BREAK IT DOWN:

- やっと finally
- あした tomorrow [kanji 明日]
- 休み【やすみ】 rest; vacation; holiday

This is casual for やっと、あしたは休【やす】みです。

NOTES:

休み is the noun form of 休む (to rest). You may also recognize it from お休み (good night).

39: Showing no sign of remorse or regret

反省の色なし
(はんせい)(いろ)
showing no sign of remorse or regret

反省の色なし

hansei no iro nashi

regret | of | the appearance | none

showing no sign of remorse or regret

BREAK IT DOWN:

- 反省【はんせい】regret; remorse

- 色【いろ】 literally means "color," but it can also mean "appearance." So, 反省の色 means "the appearance of remorse."

- ～の色【～のいろ】 the appearance of...

- なし without

NOTES:

色 (いろ) means color most of the time, but it is also used idiomatically to refer to appearances, feelings, personalities, sensuality, and tone (of one's voice).

40: The real culprit was the cat.

しんはんにん　ねこ
真犯人は猫でした。
The real culprit was the cat.

- 真犯人【しんはんにん】 the true offender
- 猫【ねこ】 cat
- でした was
- [instead of the dog everyone blamed at first]

> # 真犯人は猫でした。
>
> *shinhannin wa neko deshita.*
> real | culprit | as for | cat | was
>
> **The real culprit was the cat.**

BREAK IT DOWN:

- 真犯人【しんはんにん】the true offender
- 猫【ねこ】cat
- でした was [instead of the dog, everyone blamed at first]

NOTES:

The dog was right! 真犯人 is often used in detective shows when the first 犯人 was a red herring. Everyone thought it was the dog, but the 真犯人 was really the cat.

41: Planning a conspiracy

陰謀を計画中
planning a conspiracy

あの猫を追いかけよう！

- 陰謀【いんぼう】 conspiracy; plot; intrigue
- 計画中【けいかくちゅう】 midst of planning
- あの猫（ねこ）を追（お）いかけよう Let's chase that cat!

陰謀を計画中

inbou o keikaku chuu
conspiracy | (direct object marker) | planning | middle of (planning)

planning a conspiracy

BREAK IT DOWN:

- 陰謀【いんぼう】 conspiracy; plot; intrigue

- 計画中【けいかくちゅう】 midst of planning

- あの猫（ねこ）を追（お）いかけよう Let's chase that cat!

NOTES:

The 中 normally means "middle," but when added after nouns, it means, "while" or "in the midst of" or "during."

- 仕事中 busy working [work – middle of]
- 途中 on the way [route – middle of]
- 電話中 on the phone [phone – middle of]

42: Um? Can I help you with something?

ん？なんか用[よう]？
Um? Can I help you with something?

- ん hmm? umm? yes?
- なんか something
- 用【よう】 task; business; use; duty

> # ん？なんか用？
>
> *n? nanka you?*
> hmm? | something | business
>
> **Um? Can I help you with something?**

BREAK IT DOWN:

- ん hmm? umm? yes?

- なんか something

- 用【よう】 task; business; use; duty

NOTES:

This is a casual but common way to ask if someone needs something. Depending on the context and how it is said, it can be rude. A more polite way would be:

何^{なに}かご用^{よう}ですか？
nanika go you desu ka?
Is there something you want? (polite)

43: It's a tragedy.

ひげき

悲劇

It's a tragedy.

- 悲劇【ひげき】 tragedy; disaster
- Kanji: 悲 (grieve; sad; deplore; regret)
- Kanji: 劇 (drama; play)

悲劇
higeki
tragedy | drama

It's a tragedy.

BREAK IT DOWN:

- 悲劇【ひげき】 tragedy; disaster
- Kanji: 悲 (grieve; sad; deplore; regret)
- Kanji: 劇 (drama; play)

NOTES:

As in English, 悲劇 can be used to describe a kind of play as well as some disasterous event.

44: Cut it out. It's embarrassing.

やめて！恥ずかしいから

Cut it out. It's embarrassing.

- やめて stop it [command form of やめる (to stop)]
- 恥ずかしい【はずかしい】 embarrassed; humiliated; ashamed
- から because (it is embarrassing)

> # やめて！恥ずかしいから
>
> *yamete! hazukashii kara*
> stop it! | embarrassing | because
>
> **Cut it out. It's embarrassing.**

BREAK IT DOWN:

- やめて stop it [command form of やめる (to stop)]

- 恥ずかしい【はずかしい】 embarrassed; humiliated; ashamed

- から because (it is embarrassing)

NOTES:

This is a common construction. Give a command or conclusion followed by the explanation and から.

45: Motivated; let's play!

やる気満々
(き まんまん)

motivated

- あそぼう let's play [遊ぶ【あそぶ】(to play)]
- やる気 totally willing; fully motivated
- 満々【まんまん】full of; brimming with

> やる気満々。あそぼう！
>
> *yaruki manman. asobou!*
> motivation | full of; brimming with | let's play
>
> **Motivated; let's play!**

BREAK IT DOWN:

- あそぼう let's play [遊ぶ【あそぶ】(to play)]
- やる気 totally willing; fully motivated
- 満々【まんまん】full of; brimming with

NOTES:

やる気満々 is a common phrase for showing extreme interest.

46: Unmotivated; no will to get moving; good grief

やる気なし
Unmotivated; no will to get moving

- やれやれ oh!; ah!; oh dear!; good grief!
- やる気 totally willing; fully motivated
- なし without

やる気なし。やれやれ。

yaruki nashi. yare yare
motivation | none | oh!

Unmotivated; no will to get moving; good grief

BREAK IT DOWN:

- やれやれ oh!; ah!; oh dear!; good grief!
- やる気 totally willing; fully motivated
- なし without

NOTES:

This is the opposite of the previous entry, やる気満々 (fully motivated). やれやれ is also a common expression when tired or having to do something one doesn't want to do.

47: What should we do now?

今からどうする？
いま

What should we do now?

- 今から【いまから】 from now [今 (now) から (from)]
- どうする what to do [literally "how to do"]

今からどうする？

ima kara dou suru?
now | from | what | to do

What should we do now?

BREAK IT DOWN:

- 今から【いまから】 from now [今 (now) から (from)]
- どうする what to do [literally "how to do"]

NOTES:

This is a good phrase to use among friends. What should we do now? To make it more self-talk, you could say:

どうすればいいかな？
I wonder what I should do?

48: Not amused. Hurry up with the catnip.

つまらん。
早(はや)くまたたびくれ。
Not amused.
Hurry up with the catnip.

> つまらん。早くまたたびくれ。
>
> *tsumaran. hayaku matatabi kure.*
> boring | hurry up | catnip | please do
>
> **Not amused. Hurry up with the catnip.**

BREAK IT DOWN:

- つまらん boring; dull; uninteresting; tedious
- 早く【はやく】hurry up; quickly
- またたび catnip
- くれ please give (to me)

NOTES:

つまらん is short for つまらない (boring; tedious; dull).

49: I'm a good looking guy. Best regards!

ぼくはイケメンです。よろしく、ね！

イケメン

handsome man; a good-looking guy; a hunk

> ぼくはイケメンです。よろしく、ね！
>
> *boku wa ikemen desu. yoroshiku ne*
> I | as for | good looking guy | am | please remember me | won't you
>
> **I'm a good looking guy. Best regards!**

BREAK IT DOWN:

- ぼく I; me
- は (topic marker)
- イケメン good looking man; handsome
- です copula; am; is
- よろしく best regards; please remember me; treat me favorably; please take care of
- ね (emphatic ender; shows request for agreement)

NOTES:

A similar word to イケメン (good-looking man) is 二枚目. This literally means, "the second piece" and came from Kabuki where the second actor was the good-looking guy.

50: Anyway, hurry up and kiss me. - The prince who turned into a frog

とにかく、はやくチュウしてください。

カエルになった
おうじさま
王子様

The prince who turned into a frog

> とにかく、はやくチュウしてください。カエルになった王子様
>
> *tonikaku, hayaku chuu shite kudasai. kaeru ni natta oujisama.*
>
> anyway | hurry up | kiss | do | please | frog | became | prince
>
> **Anyway, hurry up and kiss me. - The prince who turned into a frog**

BREAK IT DOWN:

- とにかく anyway; at any rate

- はやく hurry up; quickly

- チュウ kiss

- して do (please)

- ください please (do)

- カエル frog

- になった became; turned into

- 王子様【おうじさま】 prince

- カエルになった王子様 the prince who became a frog [the main noun is the last word; the preceding phrase modifies "prince"]

> **NOTES:**

とにかく、はやく (do something) is a common way to reinforce one's previous position. Despite what you say, hurry up and do it my way anyway.

DOWNLOAD LINK

Please go to this website to download the MP3s for all stories: (There is an exclusive *free* **gift on kanji** waiting there too.)

http://japanesereaders.com/memes

Thank you for purchasing and reading this book! To contact the authors, please email them at help@thejapanshop.com. See also the wide selection of materials for learning Japanese at www.TheJapanShop.com and the free site for learning Japanese at www.TheJapanesePage.com.

Thank you for your purchase!
Did you know most of our digital ebooks are available in money-saving bundles?
Check them out at
https://www.thejapanshop.com/bundles